The Salk Institute

Photographs by Ezra Stoller

Introduction by D. S. Friedman

building blocks

Princeton Architectural Press • New York

The BUILDING BLOCKS series presents the masterworks of modern architecture through the iconic images of acclaimed architectural photographer Ezra Stoller.

Contents

Ezra Stoller

IN 1977 I DECIDED to photograph the Salk Institute on my own because it didn't look as if I'd ever be commissioned to do it, and I wanted to photograph this project, one of Lou Kahn's most important works. In the course of photographing the Institute in La Jolla, I met Dr. Salk who gave the impression that most of the ideas behind the forms were his own. And I realized that Kahn had adopted the standard architectural attitude when confronted with a powerful and opinionated client: make him think it was all his idea.

I designed a hand-held camera that used roll film and worked at my own pace, without an assitant. To me, the one element of architecture that drives the complex is time. And it has to do with the function of the human eye, perception, and the relationship of apparent vistas. There is one photograph in particular that illustrates this concept (PAGES 34–5). Spanning the interlocking voids and surfaces of Kahn's spaces, it includes at least ten vistas which the eye encompasses in a matter of nanoseconds. It would not be possible to describe the experience in words.

D. S. Friedman

LOUIS I. KAHN DESIGNED the Salk Institute for Biological Studies (1959–65) to occupy a vivid, twenty-seven-acre coastal site just above a deep cleft in the Torrey Pines mesa, overlooking the Pacific horizon. The heart of Salk is an open-ended central courtyard that divides two parallel wings, each lined along the inside face by five freestanding towers—the wings house laboratories; the towers, arcaded at the base, house private studies. In plan, labs and studies form two serrated bars that straddle the sun-baked courtyard. Standing at the entrance to this serene, open-air nave, ten thousand eyes have lifted cameras to cheekbones to record Kahn's perspective gift. A narrow ribbon of water pulls each lens due west along the courtyard's centerline, launching the viewer into a distant belt of ocean that joins the surface of the court to infinite space. Rare is the photographer, like Ezra Stoller, who not only aims and shoots, but also animates the soul of Salk's extramundane space.

Jonas Salk founded the Salk Institute for Biological Studies in 1960. Up until that time, he had been director of the Virus Research

Lab at the University of Pittsburgh, where he developed the vaccine against paralytic polio. With financial support from the National Foundation for Infantile Paralysis, sponsor of the March of Dimes, Salk proposed to gather together a new community of scientists and scholars engaged in research to prevent and cure human disease. He envisioned a kind of secular monastery for persons "from different disciplines and backgrounds" who wanted to study "the organization and processes of life."[1] Around the time Salk first met Kahn, in December 1959, he was just beginning to lay out plans for a move to California. He called Kahn on the recommendation of a friend who had heard Kahn lecture at the Carnegie Institute of Technology. During this lecture, Kahn presented work on a new medical research building for the University of Pennsylvania.

In Jonas Salk Kahn found "the most impressive intellectual [he had] ever had as a client."[2] Salk was not so much Kahn's match as his alter ego, a complementary opposite with whom Kahn shared both vision and ambition. When Salk first visited Kahn in Philadelphia, however, he knew only that he wanted to locate his new building in San Diego. He had in mind neither a site nor a program—it had been his intention merely to ask Kahn how to choose an architect. Kahn led Salk through the construction site of the Richards Medical Research Building (1957–65), but Salk was more impressed by the fifty-eight-year old architect's conversation. He offered the commission to Kahn, along with two instructions: first, he said, he needed the same amount of space as Richards, roughly 100,000 square feet; second, he said, he "would like to invite Picasso to the laboratory."

Kahn repeatedly told audiences the story about Picasso. The image of a lab fit for Picasso symbolized Salk's desire to base his scientific institute on broad, synthesizing, humanist principles. More significantly, perhaps, Kahn used it to justify his expansion of Salk's project, which quickly grew from a single building to a small campus. Over the course of their work together, which spanned six years, scientist and architect generated a personal code shaped by each other's metaphors and allusions—monastic seclusion and spirituality, peripatetic learning, the scientific and mystical body, new humanism, and the reconciliation of what C. P. Snow called the "two cultures" of science and art, which stood estranged by "a gulf of mutual incomprehension." Years later, Salk (who incidentally married Picasso's former muse, Françoise Gilot) would describe the product of his collaboration with Kahn as "a work of art to serve the work of science."[3] The Picasso story perfectly captured Salk's determination to "merge intuition and reason."[4]

From the beginning of their association onward, Salk included Kahn in formative discussions about the structure and mission of the Institute. To the extent the project had a program at all, it emerged out of their first conversations. Kahn's earliest scheme featured ungainly, prosaic towers and boxes connected by service drives that in plan looked like belted pulleys. Kahn's use of towers probably stemmed from his work on Richards, which critics lauded both for its functional clarity and for its taut, unapologetic, modern historicism. Notwithstanding international accolades (Vincent Scully called it "one of the greatest buildings of modern times"), many scientists who worked at Richards expressed disdain for Kahn's design of the labs. While Kahn likely saw this early work for Salk as a chance to set things right, Salk dismissed Kahn's first scheme as "an early fantasy."[5]

The program Kahn finally wrote described buildings divided into three primary architectural groups. Kahn's three elements included flexible, column-free laboratories, each with a ten-foot-high "servant" space and adjoining studies for scientists (Kahn's architecture of "oak table and rug"); village-like housing for Salk Institute fellows; and a meeting house, which for Kahn most represented the spiritual and philosophical purposes of the Institute. "Essentially it is

Site model showing Kahn's tripartite plan, with labs at left, scholar's residences at top right, and the proposed "meeting house" at lower right. The laboratories are the only elements to have been constructed.

a laboratory building but you must not forget that the place of meeting is almost of major importance," Kahn said of the concept behind the Institute. "These were the three kinds of spaces I thought were good for such an activity as they outlined it without any program. But in this case the architect in a way did write the program and they felt very sympathetic to it."[6]

Over the next few years, Kahn refined the designs of all three components. He located the residences west of the labs, along a gently-curving access road overlooking the southern edge of the gorge. Opposite these, on the gorge's north side, he placed an ensemble of spaces for exchange and reflection based vaguely on Hadrian's Villa. The meeting house complex—auditorium, library, dining hall, gym—remains one of Kahn's most celebrated compositions. He likened its arrangement of freestanding square and circular walls to "ruins," which he wrapped around glass-enclosed appendages to control glare.

The design of the laboratories served as a kind of middle term between the meeting house and residences. Kahn opened the base of the study towers to serve as an arcade for his courtyard plan, which in its recombination of classical parts seems most analogous to the side aisles of the Roman basilica and its various Christian successors. The idea of a courtyard and arcade, however, came not so much from an image of the basilican nave as it did Salk's image of the monastery of St. Francis in Assisi, where he stayed during a pivotal retreat in the 1950s. Salk found the ethos of St. Francis so inspiring he associated it with his break-through formulation of the poliomyelitis vaccine. Later he claimed that the final composition of the laboratories—"cloistered garden," "cortile," monastic "cells" for scientific reflection—grew out of his early conversations with Kahn about his Umbrian epiphany. More to the point, the courtyard plan embodies Kahn's unique typological inventions, which he rendered from the essential forms of these and other historical antecedents.

Kahn's second scheme stabilized the Institute's tripartite plan. It featured four two-story concrete laboratory buildings, symmetrically disposed in a plan characteristic of Kahn's early Beaux-Arts training. Each pair of laboratories flanked a central garden lined with studies. August Komendant, who worked with Kahn on the Richards Medical laboratories, engineered an innovative system of folded plates and box girders that freed the labs of columns; fully accessible, story-high mechanical spaces between the folded plates served each lab. Kahn loved this structure, but Salk abandoned the scheme within days after signing the contract for construction: he feared disunity between "'A'-court people and 'B'-court people."

Kahn modified the design accordingly, consolidating lab space into two identical six-story buildings astride a single, central garden. For this last solution, he and Komendant achieved the column-free transverse span with Vierendeel trusses, which they had employed effectively at Richards. The depth of the Vierendeels created full-height loft space for pipe and ductwork. Kahn stacked the labs and their corresponding mechanical floors three high, servant spaces atop spaces served. To preserve the scale of the courtyard, he located the bottom pair below grade. Starting at ground level, Kahn then alternated lab and study vertically: he located the studies on the second and fourth levels (the same levels as the mechanical floors), with labs on the same levels as the porch and arcade. In this dense puzzle of bridges and stairs, Kahn amplified the perception of distance between labor and contemplation. Here visitors find themselves enmeshed in the sectional logic of the building, which resolves all the paired and overlapping pieces of Kahn's vertical composition: pipe space and lab space; lab space and studies; studies and central court.

Jonas Salk, a physician and a microbiologist, read Kahn's building design in physiological terms: "The laboratories and studio [carry] the cerebral function; the service spaces [carry] the arteries, veins, and nervous system; the mechanical [spaces act] as the respiratory system . . . each integral."[7] Kahn himself adapted Salk's metaphor to describe the innovative, full-story-high 'servant space' between lab floors: "It all comes from what Dr. Salk called the *mesenchyme space*," he explained. "One serves the body, and one is the body itself."[8] This pervasive correspondence between the flesh of the wall and the flesh of the body registers most intimately in the porous space between the studies and the labs, along the primary outdoor walkways, through and beside the long arcades. Below grade, sunken gardens open the lower labs to light and air; above, open-air stairs and bridges link the porches of the studies with the balconies of the mechanical floor, which in turn shade long curtains of glass that enclose the lab spaces underneath. These interlocking volumes reveal in both form and surface what Kahn called "the record of how the building was made."

In preparation for the construction of the laboratories, Kahn immersed himself anew in the properties and qualities of concrete. He had used concrete innovatively in earlier projects—in the structure of Richards, for example, or more significantly perhaps in the ceiling of the Yale Art Gallery (1951–53). Nevertheless, he and project architect Fred Langford tested dozens of local concrete blends; they experimented with pozzuolana and other admixtures until Kahn achieved the desired consistency and volcanic color. For the formwork Kahn chose large plywood panels, a cheap but durable solution. He especially labored over the design of connections—control joints, bleed lines, even tie rod holes, which he later plugged with lead. Despite Kahn's efforts, however, the color and texture of the test pour displeased Jonas Salk. He pressed Kahn to create something "warm and alive . . . something that looked like man-made marble."[9]

Kahn tried to raise Salk's "stone" to a higher power. "If we were to train ourselves to draw as we build, from the bottom up, stopping our pencils at the joints of pouring or erecting," Kahn once wrote, "ornament would evolve out of our love for the perfection of construction and we would develop new methods of construction."[10] He left nothing to chance but the voids and tiny pockets that formed on the surface during each pour, which gave the concrete a complexion akin to travertine. For the joints, he developed small, V-shaped protrusions that expressed both the method of construction and the assiduous placement of the regulating lines of the composition. Like ornament, although rough, Kahn's seams "polish" the wall.

The focal point of this composition is of course the courtyard. But if the courtyard soothes—if it "heals"—it also unsettles. Even nowadays, thirty plus years after its completion, designers mewl about its emptiness and lack of plants or shade. Visitors and staff alike frequently note that the building's most memorable feature is its least used space, notwithstanding its stature in architectural history or its incorporation into the Institute's logo. Visiting architects recently intoned that Salk was dangerous, or irrelevant, or both: "Can a building be too strong, too special for what happens inside it? Indeed, [the architects] suggested that the environment of transcendence created at Salk inspires complacency and may even get in the way of researchers who work there."[11]

"Too strong," "too special"—too much, yet not enough: not enough trees, not ordinary enough; too much emptiness, too *spiritual*. To be sure, the composition and construction of the Salk Institute is materially direct and austere (Manfredo Tafuri called it "rigorist"). "Ideally," Kathleen James writes, "a Kahn courtyard is a place to which we come to be oriented intellectually as well as literally."[12] The courtyard at Salk far exceeds this task, as important as it is. Kahn wanted to make the laboratories *worthy of Picasso*: "I . . . saw two places, one the place of the measurable, one the place of the immeasurable."[13] If his other courtyard schemes orient occupants intellectually—at Ahmedabad or even in the central "court" of the Exeter library, for instance—Kahn's raised solar stage at Salk orients occupants spiritually, which is by his own account the primary operation of the final design.

At this stage in his career, on the threshold of international fame, Kahn grew increasingly preoccupied with the numinous presence of architecture. As work on the laboratories progressed, funding reassessments led to a new agreement between owner and architect, eliminating the construction of the meeting house and residence for fellows. When Kahn realized he might never see the meeting house completed, he transposed its "religious place"— what he called "the meeting house of the unmeasurable at the seat of the unmeasurable"—to the space between the laboratories, space still reserved for a garden. From the early garden designs, he retained the idea of a long, thin, Alhambran watercourse; but from his meeting house scheme, he imported the empty space of the peristylar square. What had been from the start a garden became in transposition an oratory.[14]

Early drawings and models show the laboratory courtyard filled with trees, doubtless a residue of the four-building version. Kahn half-heartedly iterated garden images for years. Finally, in February 1966, he flew the celebrated Mexican landscape architect Luis Barragán to the site for a two-day visit.

> I asked Barragán to come to La Jolla and help me in the choice of the planting for the garden to the Studies of the Salk Laboratory. When he entered the space he went to the concrete walls and touched them and expressed his love for them, and then said as he looked across the space and towards the sea, "I would not put a tree or blade of grass in this space. This should be a plaza of stone, not a garden." I looked at Dr. Salk and he at me and we both felt this was deeply right. Feeling our approval, he added joyously, "If you make this a plaza, you will gain a facade—a facade to the sky."[15]

Shortly after this meeting, Kahn visited Barragán in Mexico to solicit his comments on a revised courtyard plan. Salk, meanwhile, seemed wary of a solution completely devoid of plants. He and Kahn agreed to hire the well-known American landscape architect Lawrence Halprin to recommend an alternative solution. In response to Halprin's design, Kahn wrote an uncharacteristically long, carefully constructed letter to Salk, in which he argued for a new design that benefited from Halprin's ideas, but which largely followed Barragán's recommendations.

. . . . The Plaza is entirely paved with San Miguel stone which is laid tight without mortar joints. The center canal has constantly running water. The east planting encourages one to enter the Plaza from the arcades rather than to enter directly from the end. The system of narrow drainage slits tie into existing sub-surface drains and ensure positive runoff of rainwater. A broad area adjacent to the pool is surrounded by low, solid stone benches, a place to stop and enjoy the pool and the Plaza. The lower West Garden is shaded by two canopies of trees adjacent to the Office Wings.

I believe that this solution is good in bringing together the two laboratory Wings, to encourage free circulation and to inspire use and activity within the Plaza. The sensitivity of the building and this space to the many moods of the sky and the atmosphere will make the Plaza a place always changing, never static, full of the never ending anticipation of the rising and setting of the sun. . . .

. . . . In the [lower] garden, the sound of water entering a pool will take the mind from work. We realized that splashing jet fountains seen from the Laboratory associated with the utilitarian use of water would seem like mimicry. The proposed idea of the use of water, paving and potted plants will be in sympathy with the Architecture.[16]

What exactly did Kahn see, standing on the Torrey Pines mesa, gazing into the pale Pacific expanse, hand cupped over eyes against the glare? The resulting composition puts occupants in contact with a dualistic rendering of the question of life, in which "measurable" and "unmeasurable" knowledge represent two sides of the same reality. Whatever Kahn's vision, he was an architect, not a mystic. To the extent he enjoyed mystical insights, and it is certain that he did, he sought to translate these insights into built form. Yet at Salk, it is not form so much as its opposite condition, emptiness, that activates the genius of Kahn's solution. Its emptiness is neither religious nor philosophical: as Kahn often suggested, it belongs only to Architecture. If the courtyard at Salk has a poetic equivalent, surely it is a species of the kind of psychic space Wallace Stevens calls "the dumbfounding abyss between ourselves and the object, or between ourselves and other selves."[17]

Kahn interpreted Salk's vision with a house for science so strange and otherworldly that Herbert Muschamp recently called it "the most sublime landscape ever created by an American architect."[18] The unsettling power of Salk's composition in its totality of effect exceeded even Kahn's expectations. Critics agreed. Vincent Scully called Salk Kahn's "most complete and integrated work." Esther McCoy predicted that its "final revelation of forms…[would] become a part of the standard literature of architecture."[19] Many liken it to the Acropolis or Stonehenge. Others have described the regular stream of architects who visit Salk as pilgrims swarming to a shrine—one writer even compared it to Lourdes. No matter who is talking about it, all seem to say the same thing: Salk stirs the soul.

Kahn frequently quoted Wallace Stevens: "He said to the architects: What slice of the sun does your building have? And one could paraphrase by saying, what slice of the sun enters your room? As if to say, the sun never knew how great it was until it struck the side of a building."[20] Ezra Stoller has captured Salk's slice of sun. He shows us how the sun discovers its greatness on Salk's thaumaturgical surfaces. Stoller's photographs effectively document Kahn's architectural theology. If in the iconic central courtyard at Salk Kahn aims to put "the sun on trial" (to borrow one of Kahn's more provocative elocutions), Stoller aims to interpret the verdict; if at Salk Kahn uses architecture to direct the scientific eye skyward, Stoller shows us what the eye of heaven sees when it looks at Kahn's world from ground level.

1. Jonas Salk, "A Proposed Institute: A Statement [in connection with consideration by San Diego City Council of proposal to make land available . . .]," typed manuscript, March 15, 1960, "Jonas Salk," Box LIK 107, Louis I. Kahn Collection, University of Pennsylvania and Pennsylvania Historical and Museum Commission, hereafter cited as Kahn Collection.

2. David B. Brownlee, "The House of the Inspirations: Designs for Study," in David B. Brownlee and David De Long, *Louis I. Kahn: In the Realm of Architecture* (New York: Rizzoli; Los Angeles: The Museum of Contemporary Art, 1991), 95, hereafter cited as Brownlee and De Long. For a synoptic history of this project, also see Daniel S. Friedman, "Salk Institute for Biological Studies," in Brownlee and De Long, 330–338.

3. Salk, "Architecture of Reality," Louis I. Kahn Memorial Lecture, American Institute of Architects, Philadelphia, April 5, 1984, reprinted in part in *Rassegna* (March 1985): 28–29 [from "Translations of monograph," unpaginated].

4. Salk, interview with David B. Brownlee et al., April 18, 1983, tape recording transcribed by D. S. Friedman, Kahn Collection.

5. *Ibid.*, quoted in Friedman, "The Salk Institute for Biological Studies," 331.

6. "On Form and Design," speech at the 46th meeting of the Association of Collegiate Schools of Architecture, University of California at Berkeley, April 22–23, 1960, published in *The Journal of Architectural Education* 15 (Fall 1960): 62–65; reprinted in Kahn, *Louis I. Kahn: Writings, Lectures, Interviews*, ed. Alessandra Latour (New York: Rizzoli International Publications, Inc., 1991), 108, hereafter cited as *Writings*.

7. Esther McCoy, "Dr. Salk Talks about His Institute," *Architectural Forum* (December 1967): 27.

8. Kahn, from a conversation with Peter Blake, July 20, 1971, reprinted in Richard Saul Wurman, ed., *What Will Be Has Always Been: The Words of Louis I. Kahn* (New York: Access Press and Rizzoli International Publications, 1986), 130; and quoted in Friedman, "The Salk Institute," 332.

9. Salk, interview with David B. Brownlee et al., April 18, 1983.

10. Kahn, "How to Develop New Methods of Construction," *Architectural Forum* (November 1954): 157; reprinted in *Writings*, 57.

11. Thomas Hines, "The Power and Pitfalls of Greatness," *Philadelphia Inquirer* (September 2, 1984) no page number, clippings file, Kahn Collection.

12. Kathleen James, "Louis Kahn's Indian Institute of Management's Courtyard: Form versus Function," *Journal of Architectural Education* 49 (Sept. 1995): 48.

13. Kahn, "The First Robert B. Church Memorial Lecture" [February 15, 1974], *Journal of Architecture* [School of Architecture, University of Tennessee, Knoxville] (no date): 22.

14. Marco Frascari guided me to the relationship between laboratory and oratory at Salk.

15. Kahn, "Silence," *VIA* 1 (1968): 88–89; reprinted in *Writings*, 232–33.

16. Louis I. Kahn to Jonas Salk, December 19, 1966, "Salk Gardens Exedra," Box LIK, 26, Kahn Collection.

17. As paraphrased by Harold Bloom, *Kabbalah and Criticism* (New York: Seabury Press, 1975), 109.

18. Quoted in Michael Crosbie, "Add and Subtract," *Progressive Architecture* (October 1993): 48.

19. Vincent Scully, *Louis I. Kahn* (New York: George Braziller, 1962), 36; and Esther McCoy, "Buildings in the United States: 1966–1967," *Lotus* 4 (1967–68): 51.

20. Kahn, "Architecture," in *Writings*, 277.

Plates

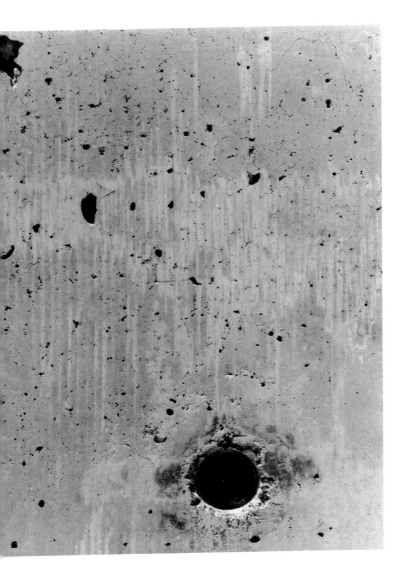

Drawings & Plans

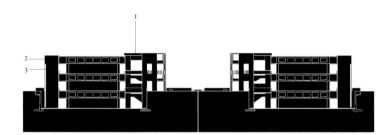

Salk Institute, cross section

1. STUDY TOWER

2. MECHANICAL LEVEL

3. LABORATORY LEVEL

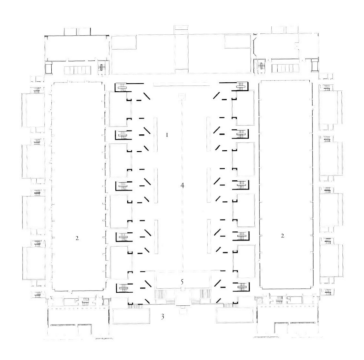

Salk Institute, courtyard level plan

1. COURTYARD

2. LABORATORY AND STUDY WINGS

3. LOWER GARDEN

4. CANAL

5. FOUNTAIN

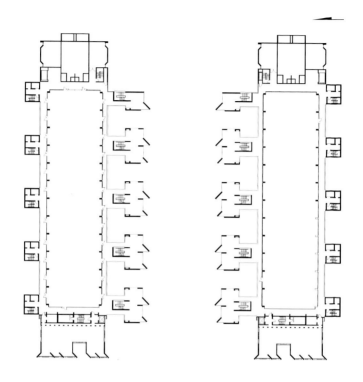

Salk Institute, plan of typical laboratory level

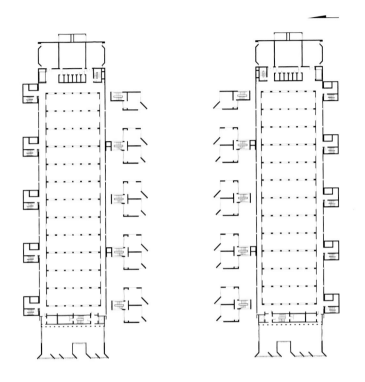

Salk Institute, plan of typical mechanical/study level

Key to Photographs

All photographs taken by Ezra Stoller in 1977.

Published by
Princeton Architectural Press
37 East Seventh Street
New York, NY 10003

For a catalog of books published by Princeton Architectural Press, call toll free 800.722.6657
or visit www.papress.com

Series editor: Mark Lamster
Project editor: Therese Kelly
Book design: Therese Kelly and Mark Lamster
Cover design: Sara E. Stemen
Drawings & plans: Kiel Moe

Acknowledgments
On behalf of my father, I would like to thank my colleagues at Esto Photographics, especially
Kent Draper and Laura Bolli; Mary Doyle and Mike Kimines of TSI Color Lab for their help
in preparing these images; and Mark Lamster for his support from start to finish.
—Erica Stoller

Princeton Architectural Press acknowledges Ann Alter, Eugenia Bell, Jan Cigliano, Jane
Garvie, Caroline Green, Beth Harrison, Clare Jacobson, Mirjana Javornik, Leslie Ann Kent,
Sara Moss, Anne Nitschke, Lottchen Shivers, Sara E. Stemen, and Jennifer Thompson
—Kevin C. Lippert, publisher

For the licensing of Ezra Stoller images, contact Esto Photographics.
Fine art reproductions of Stoller prints are available through the James Danziger Gallery.

Printed in Hong Kong.

Library of Congress Cataloging-in-Publication Data:

The Salk Institute / photographs by Ezra Stoller; introduction by Daniel S. Friedman.
        p.   cm. — (Building Blocks)
    Includes bibliographical references.
    ISBN 1-56898-200-3 (alk. paper)
    1. Salk Institute for Biological Studies. 2. Kahn, Louis I., 1901–1974 — Criticism and interpretation.
3. Research institutes — California — San Diego. 4. San Diego (California) — Buildings, structures, etc.
I. Stoller, Ezra. II. Friedman, Daniel S. III. Series: Building blocks series (New York, N.Y.)
    NA6751.S74 1999
    727'.557' 092--dc21   99-35136
                                        CIP